Poetry

from the Other Side

by

Dr. Lynn Bruce McNeely

DORRANCE
PUBLISHING CO
EST. 1920
PITTSBURGH, PENNSYLVANIA 15238

Dorrance Publishing Co
585 Alpha Drive
Pittsburgh, PA 15238
Visit our website at *www.dorrancebookstore.com*

ISBN: 979-8-88812-407-9
eISBN: 979-8-88812-907-4

Table of Contents

1 - The Night Ride 1

2 - Sitting 3

3 - Blurred Girl 4

4 - Snow 6

5 - Flu 7

6 - Home 9

7 - Pioneer Women 10

8 - The Vagrant 11

9 - Recovery 12

10 - The Creek 13

11 - Remember 14

12 - Daddy's Hands 16

13 - Cemetery Ridge 17

14 - Snow Cowboys 19

15 - The Man 20

16 - Caring 21

17 - Fitzgerald 23

18 - Life, Death and the Stream 24

19 - The Mirror 25

20 - A Still Small Voice 26

21 - The Stranger 27

22 - The Pier 28

23 - Spring 29

24 - My Birthday 30

25 - A Son's Recollection 31

26 - Golden Times 32

27 - A Day Long Ago 33

28 – Wake Up in Your Arms 34

29 - Miss Grace I 35

30 - Miss Grace II 36

31 - Where Poe Walked 38

The **Night Ride**

The woodlands trilled to the sound of the thrush
As the rider mounted his steed
And the quiet of evening settle over the fields
Now standing in saplings and weeds.

The great heavy oaks whose huge, massive arms
Were draped in Spanish mosses,
Could remember the time when soldiers in gray
Had endured here such heavy losses.

The breeze from the marsh blew warm and moist
As the rider touched his mount
And together were lost in twilight shadows
as a zephyr played about.

A mile they had ridden alone in the night
When the rider a strange chill felt
Looking over his shoulder far back down the lane
Saw a horse with light pale pelt.

The horse came on at a frightening speed
The ground seeming not to meet
The rider mottled in great tree shadows
Had a face one could not greet.

And still he came till drawing nigh
Was abreast of our riders' horse
Face still unclear in the moon's gray light
Steering a parallel course.

Now our rider asked in frightened voice,
"Who goes there beside of me?"
And a hollow sound came back on the wind,
"You're not who I took thee to be.

Ride on good friend, enjoy the night,
Drink of the evenings pure wine.
But beware of thy course in the dim twilight
Lest the pale horse becomes thine."

Sitting

Saw a crawfish earlier today
On a stream bottom surveying its' domain
And seeming to say, "Come on in, water's fine."
But snow was on the ground couple of days ago
And where was he then?
Not parading around with those big pinchers
Held so proudly skyward like a mad gardener
Showing off his shears.
No, he is a trickster. The water is cold cause
Mama said it was.
He probably heard her tell me not to get in,
Not to get wet.
He's just singing me an old crawfish song.
Not me little, Buddy. I'm gone.

Dr. Lynn Bruce McNeely

Blurred Girl

"Do you remember," she asked,
With far away eyes
Reflecting from mine,
The water of a tiny, yellow,
Plastic tub she took her
First baths in;
A small pink tricycle;
The black and white kitten
I brought her which made
Itself invisible under the car
Seat; the first bikini
she ever wore at age 3; a
tiny bit of flowered cloth over a
minute body; the cascading
marigold curls which glinted
like spun metal;
the attempts to say, "Daddy"
which came out Diddy;
the walk in the woods in
the snow when the cat
came along, hopping from
one of our tracks to the
next and meowing even
louder until I placed him
on my shoulder; the games
in the pool; the tickling;
the metamorphous
from a little girl to a
young woman; the fall
off the steps which laid open
skin to bone and the

stitches in the emergency room;
the piano recitals; joining
the church in a flowing
white dress, an ethereal beauty;
the evening I had to leave
home to not live in her
house again…
"Dad?"

Snow

The air is hushed, the sound is still
The earth is quiet below,
Limbs are burdened, bushes bent
Beneath the new laid snow.
The woods are hollow, a wonderland
By the moon's now radiant glow.
And the tracks of a fox, on his way home
Lie dimpled in the snow.
And if you walk in such a place
In its ethereal glow,
You'll hear the crunch of each footstep
As it compacts the snow.
I've never felt cold in such a place
But rather secure and snug,
As I've trod and shuffled about
On Mother Nature's rug.
I stop and think of all those things
That silence helps bring out,
And reasoning clearly, thinking anew
And push away all my doubts.
It's times like these all folk should have
For they glisten like a pearl,
They help awareness, new to bring
Of this magnificent world.

Flu

Somebody said that you've been sick
And I've been wondering why.
I've thought and thought and
Looked around, everywhere low and high.

And thinking back, I seem to recall
A lady that I knew,
Who went to call on a friend of hers,
As ladies are want to do.

She and the friend sat in the yard
While husbands went to play.
And as it is in old summer time
It got pretty hot that day.

Now trying to be a very good host
On that so hot summer day
Called for a long, cooling drink
Which under the house did lay.

The ladies brought out a couple of jars
The glass feeling cool as dew
And laying back in the warm old sun
Drank up all that home brew.

It's now been several years ago
Since that little party day.
But history surely does come around
Or so they seem to say.

I've thought about it all again,
You been out with the flu.
And I've decided, yep, I know
You found some more home brew.

Home

Where have all the flowers gone?
Where are the days of sunshine?
The sun sets now across the mountain.
The long shadows slowly consuming the pasture.
There were bells, bright lights and glittering sounds.
They cease into the shadows, perhaps to revive at sun up
      if there is to be one.
There were smiles, bright and shinning, now pale and gray,
      laughter and giggles now breezes of silence.
There was warmth, now penetrating cold. Silent cold.
A bottle, a diaper, a beach to walk in the sand. Roads, miles,
      wrinkles, tired.
Where is the part that matters?
A filamentous illusion, floating just ahead, just out of reach no
      longer beckons.
It is to join with the soil, the tree, the breeze.
Maybe I can be found there.

Dr. Lynn Bruce McNeely

*P*ioneer Woman

The sway of the horse,
Like sand through the glass thing,
Noted time.
How many miles the ride?
Down the river to the people.
The rub of bushes against my leg
As soft as a whisper, hushed, muffled,
As our thoughts were stifled
Of what we would do. Dark, silent
As the trail which led through great timber
Near the rivers' edge.
The doubled deer hides about
Our horses' hooves silently laughed as we neared.
Here in death, they cover the sounds of those
Who would snuff out life.
Were those people to live?
To steal land, deer, bear, berries, and roots?
Here is the power to hold life and death in each hand.
Some to save, some to split and skewer.
Old men to die in strife.
Babies to leave their remains
On the sharp end of a cabin log.
Excitement, riding, screaming, slitting, burning.
As we look back, the cabin corner drips.
The other cabin smolders as the flames climb.
It is too late for her to sit on a horse.
Each pounding was Pharoah's push on Moses
To go back inside.
The dark of night settled over our camp
As death had settled over their cabins.
No fire now. Dark. Heavy breaths as life was released.
From the strong woman. No sobs, no cries.

In memory of Mary Ingles

The Vagrant

The creature sat fixed to the gray
concrete as would a wet, limp leaf
which in its fall had found no
other place to go, no other option,
but to simply be.

And there would remain, as a docile,
scrawny, whale out of water, stranded on
a bleak, windswept beach, jostled
by the tide, but not moved.

And the great surging throngs radiate silence.
Unclean, stand afar off. The leprosarium.
Loneliness has dimensions, a box of life,
with walls which reach so far above that
blue sky, if there is still such a thing
is no more than a speck. There are no windows.
It is foolish to even think of a door.

Dr. Lynn Bruce McNeely

Recovery

His smile is loving, his eyes
clear and bright as a mountain's
crystal stream, reflecting a
thin moist film. The
dark circles are gone, like
shadows of a deadly night
which flee at dawn's
golden rays, bathing skin
smooth in a buttery glow.
The forehead's troubled furrows
are mellowed into a placid
plain stretched tighter at
the edges by a smile.
His mouth flows smoothly into
gentle smiles, the tight, thin lips
with turned down corners gone,
provide a window to his soul,
a soul now tons lighter.
The violence, the hatred,
the altered perceptions of walls which breathed, of street
lights which bent low to
look into his car as he
drove past; those haunting
apparitions having flown as
bats at dawn; a soul free,
light and airy, learning to
soar again, positive
thoughts, talking, warmth,
love. He is back.

The Creek

I walked today along the creek
And listened to it try to speak.
Try to say that it will not always rain
The erosion will not always be
But the rocks know better.
As they are polished, used, and discarded.
The cedars droop with water
As I walk beneath their cold arms.
They don't know me any longer
The mountain rears near the creek becoming steep
Why not?
Wet tree trunks, slick leaves, steep saturated soil
Struggle, walk on tree trunks, fall
Must move on, don't listen to the mountain's admonitions
Listen to the rain. At least it is peaceful.
A long way down now to the creek.
Straight down, rock cliff speaks.
I don't listen, I know.
Slight trickle of water crosses my path
Directing my feet to where it drops in a long,
Narrow waterfall.
I know it will be alright.

Dr. Lynn Bruce McNeely

Remember

Playing catch with your o!' Dad
Dig a hole with a big fat lad
Get a pie with red pepper hid
Return a stink bomb with a kid.

Fishing, hiking, walking alone
Memories are singing a very gray song.
Pap's chew, an odor now long gone
Wish you were here walking along.

Whisky, mules and riding cows
Sammy's gone. Not much use now.
Old hunting coat torn and drear
GOD, I wish my old man were here.
The Christmas tree in the window bright
Went outside to see its light
Fell on the steps, in arms of kin
Quarter sized hole in the edge of my shin.

High school dates, exciting and fun,
Some in the rain and some in the sun.
And evenings out late about choice or fate
Choices made now or would it be too late.

Of college days and working hard
Of pretty faces by the distance marred
Of what could have possibly been
Clearer now than possibly then.

Children's value cannot be told
A million wishes of them to hold

With pain beyond the torturer's skill
With bleeding until, until, until.

See children grown, decisions made,
Shadows now I wish could fade.
Old ones there waiting for sure,
Their fate is sealed, security assured.

Oil on water mingles and forms
Colors and hues of a life of storms
Comes a time when maybe one sees
That pursuing these forms is like chasing leaves.

Dr. Lynn Bruce McNeely

Daddy's Hands

That song Dear Ol' Daddy of Mine
Went flowing through my head
And I thought about my Daddy
And remember things that he had said.

I found an old blue scrapbook
With things of him I'd heard said.
So, sitting by an oak tree,
about him I read.

I recall at Christmas time when I ran outside to see the tree
From the yard
On the way back I took a tumble
At the time I thought I'd not grow older
But then Dad placed his hand on my young shoulder.

Daddy's hand was always there
Whenever it needed to be
Always there for soothing
Always there for me.

When I came home from Nam
Trying to figure out who I am
Trying to forget the violence
And the fires that continue
Then I felt Dad's hand resting upon my shoulder.

Then the day that had to come
When Dad's days were almost done.
I knelt by his bed
Wishing he could still grow older.
And for the very last time
He placed a feeble hand warmly on my shoulder.

Cemetery Ridge

The rain came down
like it didn't know no better.
Wonder what it would be like
to have a dry place to sleep?
The thought of dry boots is
like a bite of candy; both a dream.
Like Mama's kitchen with biscuits
on the stove, bacon frying, coffee steaming.
The sky ain't going to let up today.
Even now at daybreak there's scant
sign in the East.
We are as beat down by the rain
as with smalls packs and the heavy rifles.
I'm surprised that the damned things will even go off,
and then whether it's the weather
or the roar of thunder and cannons.
"Jake, is that you? You look like a drowned rat,
That evil slue had a bottom,
slick as hog fat. Even the horses
were slipping and falling.
What are you staring at?
You ain't said a word. There ain't nothing up ahead
sept fog and rain. You don't even seem to see me.
Jake, look at me! Jake!"
Splattering drops and sloshing boots.
"What are all your men looking at?
There ain't nothing up there.
How did we get together after that mortar attack?"
We were running wildly as stumps and men's
limbs flew past.
There are men marching without limbs.

There is no sound 'cept the sloshing. No moans.
No screams. No blood flowing.
Thirty men with fixed gaze, moving along smoothly
Not seeming to touch the ground.

Snow Cowboys

What if we could walk down underneath the snow?
Where in the world do you think that we'd go?
Underneath those shiny crystals,
Would there be snow cowboys with tiny pistols?

There would be little snow horses with long shiny tails.
All running and jumping. Their manes, they would sail.
And old snow cowboys gathering their herds.
Boy, they could tell you some exciting words.

They would tell you 'bout the time that the creek ran high,
How nowhere around was there anything dry.
How they'd piled up snow to make a great wall.
It kept the flood out and saved them all.

And sometimes at night when the moonlight abounds,
They'd come up through the snow and ride all around.
They'd play and scamper and cavort and slide.
No one can see them, in the shadows they'd hide.

Early in the morning as the sun began to glow,
They would laughingly ride back, underneath the snow.
If you'll go outside, see the clumps and the cracks,
And look very carefully, you might even see their tracks.

The Man

When I came to these mountain lands
Walked the slanted hills so covered by huge rough trunks
And dotted on the ground with Ginseng's red berry
And the May apple's yellow orb
This place began to shimmer as the sun's warm rays
Turned the frost into little clouds
Out of those mists I have met men as craggy as the hickory's coat
Men with great pirated-like coverings on their faces
Men as rough and hard as these mountains are
Which demand a price in blood to extract the black lumps lying within
A diamond, I am told, is pure carbon
Condensed by the pressure of the ages into a pure sunlight catching rock
Ever so hard, ever so ready to take a ray of light
And turn it into many shimmering shades
I met a man whose life is as blessed as the coal deposits of the ages
A man who is a part of the hills and streams, the chopping of wood
And the pounding of the black gold stones so far underground
A man who has felt GOD'S pressure and welcomed it as it turned him
Into the man GOD wanted him to be, to guide and mold him as it
Turned the coal into something beautiful, so lives in GOD'S eyes
I've had the privilege of walking through this man's past
Through the hills, streams, past the memory of a schoolhouse
And the silent invisible vestiges of his boyhood home with the strawberry
patch on the hill
And upward on another hill seventy stones who stand strong and honorable
in righteous
Testimony to those who have breathed life upon that hill one time.
Of all the beauty and wonder I have seen since coming here there has been
no thing
As dear as the wonderful man clear and meek
The gentleman I know from Cabin Creek.

Caring

If you fall and break your neck
While coming down the stairs,
Or if you catch you clothes on fire
Who in this world cares?

Oh, people will say, "I'm sorry"
Until they turn away,
Though their thoughts are somewhere else
And that is where they'll stay.

The church is always caring
Some mind numbed folks will say,
But most will close their eyes to you
While they go on to pray.

So, if you've got a problem
That prevents you from a smile,
If something has you down so bad
Just crawl on out of the isle.

The good folks have no time for you
They love you don't you know,
But if their inner thoughts were known
It's to hell where you would go.

Now the church ain't really all that bad
They've met with some success,
Their leader was after all
Truly the very best.

But its different now herein this time
Nothing's good in sight,
Maybe that leader will come back soon
To set all this crap aright.

You can look at all those people
And hear of all the war,
You can sniff up all those drugs
And stagger back for more.

And you can look for caring
But you won't find it here,
There is no room for sharing
No concern for any tear.

*F*itzgerald

Someone wrote, "Does anyone know where the love of GOD goes when the waves turn the minutes to hours?"

The stinging of the spray, where tiny salt crystals acted as invisible Cats of Nine tails, tortured us as cataclysms of wind 70 mph thundered against the ship, searching each welded seam and screamed in fury when it couldn't enter. Maybe a hatch would be the entry point we had told each other, faces white with fear, dripping, glistening, wet. Up, up we would rise on 25-foot waves then slam down throwing the taconite, the 26,000 tons of iron balls violently into the air, ricocheting them off the walls and pursuing us as though we were panicked partridges in the maw of a massive shot gun.

When the hellish storm whipped and goaded Superior into a frothing fury. It new it could isolate us from the Andersen, as a lioness separates a young gazelle from its parents, then for the kill, so did the damnable water at its height block our radar. We were alone. Alone in the wet dark, bruised, broken by the steel walls slamming against us. No controls.

The devil drives the mighty wave we cursed as it broke much above our stern and rushed brutally down the hatchway filling us. Things were more peaceful, the men's howling screams silenced. We moved more slowly now swaying in a deathly dance as she swung pendulum like ever deeper. Time, quiet time was all around us as we came to rest 525 feet down.

Dr. Lynn Bruce McNeely

*L*ife, Death, and the Stream

I sat on a rock beside my stream today,
Beside a loving Setter.
We watched, listened, smelled the breeze.
Saw rich, brown earth
Offering life to what seed
Should settle there.
Saw trees standing stark, unleafed, barren,
Many dead, ready to participate
In the recycling.
And saw smooth domed rocks
Protruding through the flowing surface
Like bald headed old men standing in a crowd.
Life, death and the stream holding hands
On a cloudy afternoon.

The **Mirror**

The old family mirror lay broken on the floor
Those tiny glass pieces not showing anymore
All the faces which had stood there looking at a friend
Now were just old memories coming back again.

Johnny used to stand there in his tiny sailor suit
And Mamma with her pride would say how very cute he looked
My little sister Sallie in her dresses standing there
How I wish I could go back and bring her now right here.

That old shining mirror where I used to play Wild Bill
And practice on my fast draw and show off all my skills.
I wish I could go back there and see them all again
To see all of my family and some of those old friends.

Sallie now is married and gone off with her Will
And Johnny's back from sailing, with uniformed service on the hill.
I stand here now in shadows coming through the open door
And look at all my life in pieces on the floor.

But there will come a time my friend when the glass will be renewed
There won't be any fractures and the faces can be viewed.
All those faces will be there just as clear as can be
Those folks from the mirror will be standing there with me.

A Still Small Voice

I stopped today by the old apple tree,
Twas a blossom out, pretty as could be.
A still small voice said, "Those colors you see?
I painted them, all for thee."
A branch higher held a tiny nest
There lay a baby sparrow at rest.
Later, as the sun began to go,
The sky filled with colors aglow
And a still small voice said to me,
"Do all these things today you see?
The blossom, the sparrow, the evening glow?
And I love them all, but do you know
That I love you more than all their glow?
Said a still small voice.

The Stranger

Twas a gray rainy day
December in Caroline.
Scant weeks ahead of Christmas
With all the glitter and shine.

I walked down the marble hall
A deacon here, proud to be.
Saw a man standing
Where no one was supposed to be.

He was slim and taller than me,
A brown coat and hood he wore.
Standing where no one was supposed to be
He approached me from the door.

"I need some money," he said to me.
I'm afraid he turned me off.
Why's he not where he is supposed to be
Inside, I felt a scoff.

Something was different about this man
With strong nose and piercing eyes.
But of beggars I was never a fan,
Had never heard their cries.

"How much money you want?"
I said with a sigh.
"Not much, maybe five bucks.
Just for a long bus ride."

The Pier

The ocean is still, unusual it seems,
Quiet and peaceful with an alluring appeal.
The boardwalk above is rough and blotched
Where insides of fish have stained and flopped.
The walkway sways ever so softly as the
Huge swells pass below.
We loved to walk there, to go to the end,
Put our arms on the top railing and gaze out into
A fabled world where surely Edward Teach had sailed past
In a time where violence was as rampant at sea
As now on dry land.
We would talk about the mysteries that lay beneath the surface
The monster fish which disappear a human so quickly
And leave no trace.
We would adjust the tension on our lives, dreading
One of the behemoths.
Then with none in tow, stand side-by-side eyeing the water
With an arm about each other's shoulders
He loved this spot, the beach, this pier.
To what better place to bring him from which he need not return.
In the sea, which he loved, underneath it where he resides.
I come here often to be with him, to listen to his
Strong words, to lean upon his iron shoulders
And tell him how very much I miss and love him.

Spring

A post stands at the edge of the pasture
Inviting some to sit and lean a while.
Mint is starting to grow and give life
To odors which take flight
And do magical things to the air.
Dimples abound in the soft brown earth.
Their makers come by and look at me
Their brown eyes asking why I sit by their post.
Robins have returned, an action which in harmony with the mint
Elevates the soul.
On the mountain, atop the highest tree,
Two golden eagles sit at the edge of their nest
And daydream of their clutch.
At the tree base, ramps begin to point their tips
Through the leaves.
Indian paint brush and wild ginger compete for attention.
Look and live with me they say.

My Birthday

So, today's, the day that I turn… something,
I guess I should go on and say it.
But then, maybe it's not important,
So, I think I'm just going to skip it.

Kathy tells me that you're as young as you feel,
But I know that to be plain wrong.
Cause there are things that I used to could do,
And now they're just plain gone.

Kathy says the way I tilt back my head
That I look like a snobbish yokel.
Fact is, I have to tilt back my head
To see through these darned bifocals.

The TV tells me to do exercise
To get down there and work out.
I never realized that just getting back up
Required you to be darned stout.

A Son's Recollections

When I was young my Dad was not what I thought he should be.
Much later he said that things at home had changed his ability to see.
After he left, I lost the faith in him that I used to hold,
Mostly because of what Mamma on every occasion told.
If I could just see him again, I'd hug him ever so dear,
And tell him I'm sorry I didn't hold him ever so near.
And yet he was there whenever I had called
I just couldn't forget that day back in the fall when we walked
Through the corn field and I told him I had to leave.
I never understood how much the old man grieved.
Later he heard me say, "It was leave or die from all the hell at home."
I didn't understand until I was almost grown
By then from all that I'd been told I didn't know who to believe,
I just went my way not knowing how much the old man grieved.
He'd say that when finally gone the family would rejoice,
But now as I look back at him, I wish I had the choice
To hold him close and hear again his very wise old voice.

Dr. Lynn Bruce McNeely

Golden Times

We're gathered here today for what is it we shall say
To celebrate something for which I had nothing to do,
I know that and so do you.
We're gathered here to dine and sup
All I had to do was just show up.
Fact is that all these years of which we fear
All I did was just be here.
But then there's this thing of getting old
It's pretty rough so I've been told.
Things that use to work ever so fair
Now don't, so I won't even go there.
Like once I used to have beautiful hair
Now I don't except here and there.
Of those places, have I not chose
Tis hair in my ears and growing out of my nose.
Now remembering has become quite an affair
I start off but can't figure why I'm going there.
When I get there for whatever or where
I try to figure just how I got there.
Oh well, I just start back toward home
And then wander and wander and wander and roam.
But birthdays are great and I hear one is near
But now why is it that all of you are here?

A Day Long Ago

Shadows grow long at the end of the way
Memories drift back to an earlier day
When kids were in diapers and feeding at night
And peeing on you, but it was alright.

A little pink bike shines in my night
Pens under the bed bound up tight
Beautiful curls and a yellow gauze dress
Ephemeral image Monet to impress.

Shadows were so awfully short then
Never thought of a future when
They'd have grown so much longer
But put on muscle and become stronger.

Struggle my sanity to reinforce
Fighting upstream you find of course
Can prayer really turn it back
It feeds on itself and gives no slack.

Dr. Lynn Bruce McNeely

Wake Up in Your Arms

When I got out of prison, I had nothing that was mine
And I couldn't have cared less, just wasted all that time.
Soon I started riding hard with old boys left behind,
We thundered on those scooters, those sure were the times.

But something big was missing, gnawing at my soul,
Something a man needs, something to make him whole.
Back when I had left here, I was working on our farm,
It was her I wanted back, to wake up in her arms.

When we lost our little boy that cold November day,
His little heart just wouldn't beat right was all that they would say.
That set off such pain in me like a terrible raging storm,
All I wanted was the peace of waking up in his arms.

I realized I'd have to pray my LORD would throw me a rope,
Something from the past that would at least give me hope.
Something HE would give me, maybe to keep me warm,
Cause now when I wake up, I want to be there is His arms.

Waking in Your arms is all I could desire
It would bring me some peace from all the smoldering fire.
My heart so awfully empty needed filling to the brim,
Only place I could return was once again to Him.

Miss Grace I

On this grand and anticipated moment
When we look forward to joys to come,
There surely must be a commemorating comment
Which for years will be remembered by some.

On this lovely morning adorned by light
We await a young lady to enter our life,
Who will equal the morning in radiance so bright
And wish for years free of all strife.

And if a magic wand were mine
That I could wield with power,
She would not be touched by time
But grow more radiant by the hour.

Grace, I'm told is to be her name
And a lovely name indeed,
One that will crown her with its fame
And wipe away every need.

Dr. Lynn Bruce McNeely

Miss Grace II

Precious One, I can't believe you are two
Doesn't seem that long since I first heard of you
Saw your mom then, couple of years back
Looked like you two were right on track

Heard you had a poem, read to you back when
By some old lady happening by when
She heard of this baby that was due any day
And had to stop in just to say, "Hey."

Since then, you've grown and gotten so cute
And eat all your vegetables and all of your fruit
And chase the dogs and pull their tails
And think of possibilities with hammer and nails.

The pictures you draw are at least like Van Gogh
And even though Mommy say they really must go
I think they are art works, each one, all
Even when they are on the dining room wall

And socks, why they weren't made to wear
But to be lost and hidden anywhere.
And why does my it have to change more on my mood
When you're only playing with ol' Norman's food?

Yeah, I see in that crystal ball of mine
A pretty young lady, growing so fine
And having installed her own telephone line
And all the boys saying, "Wish Grace were mine."

But 'tween now and then we've got a few years
To party like this and drink some beers,
And to open the boxes and have lots of fun,
And get a bikini and lay in the sun.

But of all of those people who so envious will be
Of a pretty little girl to sit upon their knee
I can tell you right now and my words will be free
No one will, any more than me.

Dr. Lynn Bruce McNeely

Where Poe Walked

Wet sand shaped into a mold
For the shiny silver it would soon hold.
A straight shaft with a handle and cross
Quietly it fit my hand at a loss.

My steps sounded loud on the damp sidewalk.
Echoing along cobblestones. There was no talk.
The lamps were lit and the moths drew near,
No one's out in this hour of fear.

London's streets were mottled with light,
I stayed in shadows well out of sight.
An hour's walk through the retched slums,
No one from their door had come.

Midnight had fled when turning the street
A very old man, I happened to see,
Plodding along it appeared to me.
Head held down, a sad sight to see.

I gradually drew near him
But did not pass upon a whim.
Two paces behind I followed him;
Lamplight made his old skin dim.

As he walked his arm swung back,
Showing the place where I would attack.
Next step, my arms around him
And I gasping, he was so thin.

Rapidly I slid the silver blade
From my hand where it had lain.
Incredibly, no sound he made,
But the pace of his walk began to fade.

At the lamp, I passed him by
He reached out as if to try
To catch the post, but he
Slipped down quietly, like a ghost.

Further I saw from a blackened tree
He was poised, quietly, down on one knee.
A block farther he was on his face
Yet silence still held in place.

Thinking, I have surely decided
Another hour and the Town Cryer
Would be the morning lark.
Yes, it should be a lovely day in the park.

www.ingramcontent.com/pod-product-compliance
Lightning Source LLC
Chambersburg PA
CBHW061646130726
47996CB00003B/1473